TRUE WEST

by the same author

TRUE WEST

SAM SHEPARD

FABER AND FABER

LONDON   BOSTON

First published in 1981
by Faber and Faber Limited
3 Queen Square London WC1N 3AU
Printed in Great Britain by
Latimer Trend & Company Ltd Plymouth
All rights reserved

British Library Cataloguing in Publication Data

Shepard, Sam
True West.
I. Title
812'.54   PS3537.H/

ISBN 0-571-11833-x

CHARACTERS

AUSTIN: Early thirties, light blue sports shirt, light tan cardigan sweater, clean blue jeans, white tennis shoes

LEE: His older brother, early forties, filthy white T-shirt, tattered brown overcoat covered with dust, dark blue baggy suit pants from the Salvation Army, pink suede belt, pointed black forties' dress-shoes scuffed up, holes in the soles, no socks, no hat, long pronounced sideburns, 'Gene Vincent' hairdo, two days' growth of beard, bad teeth

SAUL KIMMER: Late forties, Hollywood producer, pink and white flower-print sports shirt, white sports coat with matching polyester slacks, black and white loafers

MOM: Early sixties, mother of the brothers, small woman, conservative white skirt and matching jacket, red shoulder bag, two pieces of matching red luggage

The first performance of *True West* was given at The National Theatre on 23 November 1981 and was directed by John Schlesinger.

SET

All nine scenes take place on the same set; a kitchen and adjoining alcove of an older home in a Southern California suburb, about forty miles east of L.A. The kitchen takes up the majority of the playing area to stage left (from the actor's point of view, facing the audience). The kitchen consists of a sink, up stage center, surrounded by counter space, a wall telephone, cupboards and a small window just above it bordered by neat yellow curtains. Stage left of sink is a stove. Stage right, a refrigerator. The alcove adjoins the kitchen to stage right. There is no wall division or door to the alcove. It is open and easily accessible from the kitchen and defined only by the objects in it: a small, round, glass breakfast table mounted on white iron legs; two matching white iron chairs set across from each other. The two exterior walls of the alcove which prescribe a corner in the up stage right are composed of many small windows beginning from a solid wall about three feet high and extending to the ceiling. The windows look out to bushes and citrus trees. The alcove is filled with all sorts of house plants in various pots, mostly Boston ferns hanging in planters at different levels. The floor of the alcove is composed of green synthetic grass.

All entrances and exits are made stage left from the kitchen. There is no door. The actors simply go off and come onto the playing area.

NOTE ON SET AND COSTUME

The set should be constructed realistically with no attempt to distort its dimensions, shapes, objects or colors. No objects should be introduced which might draw special attention to themselves other than the props demanded by the script. If a stylistic 'concept' is grafted onto the set design it will only serve to confuse the evolution of the characters' situation, which is the most important focus of the play.

Likewise, the costumes should be exactly representative of who the characters are, and not added onto for the sake of making a point to the audience.

NOTE ON SOUND

The Coyote of Southern California has a distinct yapping, dog-like bark, similar to a Hyena. This yapping grows more intense and maniacal as the pack grows in numbers, which is usually the case when they lure and kill pets from suburban yards. The sense of growing frenzy in the pack should be felt in the background, particularly in Scenes Seven and Eight. In any case, these Coyotes never make the long, mournful, solitary howl of the Hollywood stereotype.

The sound of Crickets can speak for itself.

These sounds should also be treated realistically even though they sometimes grow in volume and numbers.

ACT ONE

SCENE ONE

Night, sound of crickets in dark, candlelight appears in alcove illuminating AUSTIN *seated at glass table, hunched over a writing notebook, pen in hand, cigarette burning in ashtray, cup of coffee, typewriter on table, stacks of paper, candle burning on table.*

Soft moonlight fills kitchen, illuminating LEE, *beer in hand, six pack on counter behind him, he's leaning against sink, mildly drunk, takes slug of beer.*

LEE: So, Mom took off for Alaska, huh?

AUSTIN: Yeah.

LEE: Sorta' left you in charge.

AUSTIN: Well, she knew I was coming down here so she offered me the place.

LEE: You keepin' the plants watered?

AUSTIN: Yeah.

LEE: Keepin' the sink clean? She don't like even a single tea leaf in the sink ya' know.

AUSTIN: *(Trying to concentrate on writing)* Yeah, I know.
(Pause)

LEE: She gonna' be up there a long time?

AUSTIN: I don't know.

LEE: Kinda' nice for you, huh? Whole place to yourself.

AUSTIN: Yeah, it's great.

LEE: Ya' got crickets anyway. Tons a' crickets out there. *(Looks around kitchen.)* Ya' got groceries? Coffee?

AUSTIN: *(Looking up from writing)* What?

LEE: You got coffee?

AUSTIN: Yeah.

LEE: 'At's good. *(Short pause.)* Real coffee? From the bean?

AUSTIN: Yeah. You want some?

LEE: Naw. I brought some uh— *(Motions to beer.)*

9

AUSTIN: Help yourself to whatever's— (*Motions to refrigerator.*)

LEE: I will. Don't worry about me. I'm not the one to worry about. I mean I can uh— (*Pause*) You always work by candlelight?

AUSTIN: No—uh— Not always.

LEE: Just sometimes?

AUSTIN: (*Puts pen down, rubs his eyes*) Yeah. Sometimes it's soothing.

LEE: Isn't that what the old guys did?

AUSTIN: What old guys?

LEE: The Forefathers. You know.

AUSTIN: Forefathers?

LEE: Isn't that what they did? Candlelight burning into the night? Cabins in the wilderness.

AUSTIN: (*Rubs hand through his hair*) I suppose.

LEE: I'm not botherin' you am I? I mean I don't wanna break into yer uh—concentration or nothin'.

AUSTIN: No, it's all right.

LEE: That's good. I mean I realize that yer line a' work demands a lota' concentration.

AUSTIN: It's okay.

LEE: You probably think that I'm not fully able to comprehend somethin' like that, huh?

AUSTIN: Like what?

LEE: That stuff yer doin'. That art. You know. Whatever you call it.

AUSTIN: It's just a little research.

LEE: You may not know it but I did a little art myself once.

AUSTIN: You did?

LEE: Yeah! I did some a' that. I fooled around with it. No future in it.

AUSTIN: What'd you do?

LEE: Never mind what I did! Just never mind about that. (*Pause*) It was ahead of its time.

(*Pause*)

AUSTIN: So, you went out to see the old man, huh?

LEE: Yeah, I seen him.

AUSTIN: How's he doing?

LEE: Same. He's doin' just about the same.

AUSTIN: I was down there too, you know.

LEE: What d'ya' want, an award? You want some kinda' medal? You were down there. He told me all about you.

AUSTIN: What'd he say?

LEE: He told me. Don't worry.

(Pause)

AUSTIN: Well—

LEE: You don't have to say nothin'.

AUSTIN: I wasn't.

LEE: Yeah, you were gonna' make somethin' up. Somethin' brilliant.

(Pause)

AUSTIN: You going to be down here very long, Lee?

LEE: Might be. Depends on a few things.

AUSTIN: You got some friends down here?

LEE: (Laughs) I know a few people. Yeah.

AUSTIN: Well, you can stay here as long as I'm here.

LEE: I don't need your permission do I?

AUSTIN: No.

LEE: I mean she's my mother too, right?

AUSTIN: Right.

LEE: She might've just as easily asked me to take care of her place as you.

AUSTIN: That's right.

LEE: I mean I know how to water plants.

(Long pause.)

AUSTIN: So you don't know how long you'll be staying then?

LEE: Depends mostly on houses, ya' know.

AUSTIN: Houses?

LEE: Yeah. Houses. Electric devices. Stuff like that. I gotta' make a little tour first.

(Short pause.)

AUSTIN: Lee, why don't you just try another neighborhood, all right?

LEE: (Laughs) What'sa' matter with this neighborhood? This is a great neighborhood. Lush. Good class a' people. Not many dogs.

11

AUSTIN: Well, our uh— Our mother just happens to live here. That's all.

LEE: Nobody's gonna' know. All they know is somethin's missing. That's all. She'll never even hear about it. Nobody's gonna' know.

AUSTIN: You're going to get picked up if you start walking around here at night.

LEE: Me? I'm gonna, git picked up? What about you? You stick out like a sore thumb. Look at you. You think yer regular lookin'?

AUSTIN: I've got too much to deal with here to be worrying about—

LEE: Yer not gonna' have to worry about me! I've been doin' all right without you. I haven't been anywhere near you for five years! Now isn't that true?

AUSTIN: Yeah.

LEE: So you don't have to worry about me. I'm a free agent.

AUSTIN: All right.

LEE: Now all I wanna' do is borrow yer car.

AUSTIN: No!

LEE: Just fer a day. One day.

AUSTIN: No!

LEE: I won't take it outside a twenty-mile radius. I promise ya'. You can check the speedometer.

AUSTIN: You're not borrowing my car! That's all there is to it.
(*Pause*)

LEE: Then I'll just take the damn thing.

AUSTIN: Lee, look— I don't want any trouble, all right?

LEE: That's a dumb line. That is a dumb fuckin' line. You git paid fer dreamin' up a line like that?

AUSTIN: Look, I can give you some money if you need money.
(LEE *suddenly lunges at* AUSTIN, *grabs him violently by the shirt, and shakes him with tremendous power.*)

LEE: Don't you say that to me! Don't you ever say that to me!
(*Just as suddenly* LEE *turns* AUSTIN *loose, pushes him away and backs off.*)
You may be able to git away with that with the old man.

12

Git him tanked up for a week! Buy him off with yer Hollywood blood money, but not me! I can git my own money my own way. Big money!

AUSTIN: I was just making an offer.

LEE: Yeah, well keep it to yourself! (*Long pause.*) Those are the most monotonous fuckin' crickets I ever heard in my life.

AUSTIN: I kinda' like the sound.

LEE: Yeah. Supposed to be able to tell the temperature by the number a' pulses. You believe that?

AUSTIN: The temperature?

LEE: Yeah. The air. How hot it is.

AUSTIN: How do you do that?

LEE: I don't know. Some woman told me that. She was a Botanist. So I believed her.

AUSTIN: Where'd you meet her?

LEE: What?

AUSTIN: The woman Botanist?

LEE: I met her on the desert. I been spendin' a lota' time on the desert.

AUSTIN: What were you doing out there?

LEE: (*Pause, stares in space*) I forgit. Had me a Pit Bull there for a while but I lost him.

AUSTIN: Pit Bull?

LEE: Fightin' dog. Damn, I made some good money off that little dog. Real good money.
(*Pause*)

AUSTIN: You could come up north with me, you know.

LEE: What's up there?

AUSTIN: My family.

LEE: Oh, that's right, you got the wife and kiddies now don't ya'. The house, the car, the whole slam. That's right.

AUSTIN: You could spend a couple days. See how you like it. I've got an extra room.

LEE: Too cold up there.
(*Pause*)

AUSTIN: You want to sleep for a while?

LEE: (*Pause, stares at* AUSTIN) I don't sleep.
(*Lights to black.*)

13

SCENE TWO

Morning, AUSTIN *is watering plants with a vaporizer,* LEE *sits at glass table in alcove drinking beer.*

LEE: I never realized the old lady was so security-minded.

AUSTIN: How do you mean?

LEE: Made a little tour this morning. She's got locks on everything. Locks and double-locks and chain-locks and— What's she got that's so valuable?

AUSTIN: Antiques I guess. I don't know.

LEE: Antiques! Brought everything with her from the old place, huh. Just the same crap we always had around. Plates and spoons.

AUSTIN: I guess they have personal value to her.

LEE: Personal value. Yeah. Just a lota' junk. Most of it's phony anyway. Idaho decals. Now who in the hell wants to eat offa' plate with the State of Idaho starin' ya' in the face. Every time ya' take a bite ya' get to see a little bit more.

AUSTIN: Well it must mean something to her or she wouldn't save it.

LEE: Yeah, well personally I don't wanna' be invaded by Idaho when I'm eatin'. When I'm eatin' I'm home. Ya' know what I'm sayin'? I'm not driftin', I'm home. I don't need my thoughts swept off to Idaho. I don't need that!
(*Pause*)

AUSTIN: Did you go out last night?

LEE: Why?

AUSTIN: I thought I heard you go out.

LEE: Yeah, I went out. What about it?

AUSTIN: Just wondered.

LEE: Damn coyotes kept me awake.

AUSTIN: Oh yeah, I heard them. They must've killed somebody's dog or something.

LEE: Yappin' their fool heads off. They don't yap like that on the desert. They howl. These are city coyotes here.

14

AUSTIN: Well, you don't sleep anyway do you?
(*Pause,* LEE *stares at him.*)
LEE: You're pretty smart aren't ya'?
AUSTIN: How do you mean?
LEE: I mean you never had any more on the ball than I did. But
here you are gettin' invited into prominent people's houses.
Sittin' around talkin' like you know somethin'.
AUSTIN: They're not so prominent.
LEE: They're a helluva' lot more prominent than the houses I get
invited into.
AUSTIN: Well you invite yourself.
LEE: That's right. I do. In fact I probably got a wider range a'
choices than you do, come to think of it.
AUSTIN: I wouldn't doubt it.
LEE: In fact I been inside some pretty classy places in my time.
And I never even went to an Ivy League school either.
AUSTIN: You want some breakfast or something?
LEE: Breakfast?
AUSTIN: Yeah. Don't you eat breakfast?
LEE: Look, don't worry about me pal. I can take care a' myself.
You just go ahead as though I wasn't even here, all right?
(AUSTIN *goes into kitchen, makes coffee.*)
AUSTIN: Where'd you walk to last night?
(*Pause*)
LEE: I went up in the foothills there. Up in the San Gabriels.
Heat was drivin' me crazy.
AUSTIN: Well, wasn't it hot out on the desert?
LEE: Different kinda' heat. Out there it's clean. Cools off at
night. There's a nice little breeze.
AUSTIN: Where were you, the Mojave?
LEE: Yeah. The Mojave. That's right.
AUSTIN: I haven't been out there in years.
LEE: Out past Needles there.
AUSTIN: Oh yeah.
LEE: Up here it's different. This country's real different.
AUSTIN: Well, it's been built up.
LEE: Built up? Wiped out is more like it. I don't even hardly
recognize it.

AUSTIN: Yeah. Foothills are the same though, aren't they?

LEE: Pretty much. It's funny goin' up in there. The smells and everything. Used to catch snakes up there, remember?

AUSTIN: You caught snakes.

LEE: Yeah. And you'd pretend you were Geronimo or some damn thing. You used to go right out to lunch.

AUSTIN: I enjoyed my imagination.

LEE: That what you call it? Looks like yer still enjoyin' it.

AUSTIN: So you just wandered around up there, huh?

LEE: Yeah. With a purpose.

AUSTIN: See any houses?

(*Pause*)

LEE: Couple. Couple a' real nice ones. One of 'em didn't even have a dog. Walked right up and stuck my head in the window. Not a peep. Just a sweet kinda' suburban silence.

AUSTIN: What kind of a place was it?

LEE: Like a paradise. Kinda' place that sorta' kills ya' inside. Warm yellow lights. Mexican tile all around. Copper pots hangin' over the stove. Ya' know like they got in the magazines. Blond people movin' in and outa' the rooms, talkin' to each other. (*Pause*) Kinda place you wish you'd sorta' grew up in, ya' know.

AUSTIN: That's the kind of place you wish you'd grown up in?

LEE: Yeah, why not?

AUSTIN: I thought you hated that kind of stuff.

LEE: Yeah, well you never knew too much about me did ya'?

(*Pause*)

AUSTIN: Why'd you go out to the desert in the first place?

LEE: I was on my way to see the old man.

AUSTIN: You mean you just passed through there?

LEE: Yeah. That's right. Three months of passin' through.

AUSTIN: Three months?

LEE: Somethin' like that. Maybe more. Why?

AUSTIN: You lived on the Mojave for three months?

LEE: Yeah. What'sa' matter with that?

AUSTIN: By yourself?

LEE: Mostly. Had a couple a' visitors. Had that dog for a while.

AUSTIN: Didn't you miss people?

16

LEE: (*Laughs*) People?

AUSTIN: Yeah. I mean I go crazy if I have to spend three nights in a motel by myself.

LEE: Yer not in a motel now.

AUSTIN: No, I know. But sometimes I have to stay in motels.

LEE: Well, they got people in motels don't they?

AUSTIN: Strangers.

LEE: Yer friendly aren't ya'? Aren't you the friendly type?

(*Pause*)

AUSTIN: I'm going to have somebody coming by here later, Lee.

LEE: Ah! Lady friend?

AUSTIN: No, a producer.

LEE: Aha! What's he produce?

AUSTIN: Film. Movies. You know.

LEE: Oh, movies. Motion Pictures! A Big Wig huh?

AUSTIN: Yeah.

LEE: What's he comin' by here for?

AUSTIN: We have to talk about a project.

LEE: Whadya' mean, 'a project'? What's 'a project'?

AUSTIN: A script.

LEE: Oh. That's what yer doin' with all these papers?

AUSTIN: Yeah.

LEE: Well, what's the project about?

AUSTIN: We're uh— It's a period piece.

LEE: What's 'a period piece'?

AUSTIN: Look, it doesn't matter. The main thing is we need to discuss this alone. I mean—

LEE: Oh, I get it. You want me outa' the picture.

AUSTIN: Not exactly. I just need to be alone with him for a couple of hours. So we can talk.

LEE: Yer afraid I'll embarrass ya' huh?

AUSTIN: I'm not afraid you'll embarrass me!

LEE: Well, I tell ya' what— Why don't you just gimme the keys to yer car and I'll be back around six o'clock or so. That give ya enough time?

AUSTIN: I'm not loaning you my car, Lee.

LEE: You want me to just git lost, huh? Take a hike? Is that it? Pound the pavement for a few hours while you bullshit yer way into a million bucks.

AUSTIN: Look, it's going to be hard enough for me to face this character on my own without—

LEE: You don't know this guy?

AUSTIN: No I don't know— He's a producer. I mean I've been meeting with him for months but you never get to know a producer.

LEE: Yer tryin' to hustle him? Is that it?

AUSTIN: I'm not trying to hustle him! I'm trying to work out a deal! It's not easy.

LEE: What kinda' deal?

AUSTIN: Convince him it's a worthwhile story.

LEE: He's not convinced? How come he's comin' over here if he's not convinced? I'll convince him for ya'.

AUSTIN: You don't understand the way things work down here.

LEE: How do things work down here?

   (*Pause*)

AUSTIN: Look, if I loan you my car will you have it back here by six?

LEE: On the button. With a full tank a' gas.

AUSTIN: (*Digging in his pocket for keys*) Forget about the gas.

LEE: Hey, these days gas is gold, old buddy.

   (AUSTIN *hands the keys to* LEE.)

   You remember that car I used to loan you?

AUSTIN: Yeah.

LEE: Forty Ford. Flathead.

AUSTIN: Yeah.

LEE: Sucker hauled ass didn't it?

AUSTIN: Lee, it's not that I don't want to loan you my car—

LEE: You are loanin' me yer car.

   (LEE *gives* AUSTIN *a pat on the shoulder. Pause*)

AUSTIN: I know. I just wish—

LEE: What? You wish what?

AUSTIN: I don't know. I wish I wasn't— I wish I didn't have to be doing business down here. I'd like to just spend some time with you.

LEE: I thought it was 'Art' you were doin'.

   (LEE *moves across the kitchen toward exit, tosses keys in his hand.*)

AUSTIN: Try to get it back here by six, okay?

LEE: No sweat. Hey, ya' know, if that uh—story of yours doesn't go over with the guy—tell him I got a couple a' 'projects' he might be interested in. Real commercial. Full a' suspense. True-to-life stuff.

(LEE *exits,* AUSTIN *stares after him then turns, goes to papers at table, leafs through pages, lights fade to black.*)

SCENE THREE

Afternoon, alcove, SAUL KIMMER *and* AUSTIN *seated across from each other at table.*

SAUL: Well, to tell you the truth, Austin, I have never felt so confident about a project in quite a long time.

AUSTIN: Well, that's good to hear, Saul.

SAUL: I am absolutely convinced we can get this thing off the ground. I mean we'll have to make a sale to television and that means getting a major star. Somebody bankable. But I think we can do it. I really do.

AUSTIN: Don't you think we need a first draft before we approach a star?

SAUL: No, no, not at all. I don't think it's necessary. Maybe a brief synopsis. I don't want you to touch the typewriter until we have some seed money.

AUSTIN: That's fine with me.

SAUL: I mean it's a great story. Just the story alone. You've really managed to capture something this time.

AUSTIN: I'm glad you like it, Saul.

(LEE *enters abruptly into kitchen carrying a stolen television set. Short pause.*)

LEE: Aw shit, I'm sorry about that. I am really sorry, Austin.

AUSTIN: (*Standing*) That's all right.

LEE: (*Moving toward them*) I mean I thought it was way past six already. You said to have it back here by six.

AUSTIN: We were just finishing up. (*To* SAUL.) This is my uh—

brother, Lee.

SAUL: (*Standing*) Oh, I'm very happy to meet you.

(LEE *sets TV on sink counter, shakes hands with* SAUL.)

LEE: I can't tell ya' how happy I am to meet you, sir.

SAUL: Saul Kimmer.

LEE: Mr Kipper.

SAUL: Kimmer.

AUSTIN: Lee's been living out on the desert and he just uh—

SAUL: Oh, that's terrific! (*To* LEE.) Palm Springs?

LEE: Yeah. Yeah, right. Right around in that area. Near uh—Bob Hope Drive there.

SAUL: Oh I love it out there. I just love it. The air is wonderful.

LEE: Yeah. Sure is. Healthy.

SAUL: And the golf. I don't know if you play golf, but the golf is just about the best.

LEE: I play a lota' golf.

SAUL: Is that right?

LEE: Yeah. In fact I was hoping I'd run into somebody out here who played a little golf. I've been lookin' for a partner.

SAUL: Well, I uh—

AUSTIN: Lee's just down for a visit while our mother's in Alaska.

SAUL: Oh, your mother's in Alaska?

AUSTIN: Yes. She went up there on a little vacation. This is her place.

SAUL: I see. Well isn't that something. Alaska.

LEE: What kinda' handicap do ya' have, Mr Kimmer?

SAUL: Oh I'm just a Sunday duffer really. You know.

LEE: That's good 'cause I haven't swung a club in months.

SAUL: Well we ought to get together sometime and have a little game. Austin, do you play? (SAUL *mimes a Johnny Carson golf swing for* AUSTIN.)

AUSTIN: No. I don't uh— I've watched it on TV.

LEE: (*To* SAUL) How 'bout tomorrow morning? Bright and early. We could get out there and put in eighteen holes before breakfast.

SAUL: Well, I've got uh— I have several appointments—

LEE: No, I mean real early. Crack a' dawn. While the dew's still thick on the fairway.

20

SAUL: Sounds really great.

LEE: Austin could be our caddie.

SAUL: Now that's an idea. (*Laughs*)

AUSTIN: I don't know the first thing about golf.

LEE: There's nothin' to it. Isn't that right, Saul? He'd pick it up in fifteen minutes.

SAUL: Sure. Doesn't take long. 'Course you have to play for years to find your true form. (*Chuckles*)

LEE: (*To* AUSTIN) We'll give ya' a quick run-down on the club faces. The irons, the woods. Show ya' a couple pointers on the basic swing. Might even let ya' hit the ball a couple times. Whadya' think, Saul?

SAUL: Why not. I think it'd be great. I haven't had any exercise in weeks.

LEE: 'At's the spirit! We'll have a little orange juice right afterwards.

(*Pause*)

SAUL: Orange juice?

LEE: Yeah! Vitamin C! Nothin' like a shot a' orange juice after a round a' golf. Hot shower. Snappin' towels at each other's privates. Real sense a' fraternity.

SAUL: (*Smiles at* AUSTIN) Well, you make it sound very inviting, I must say. It really does sound great.

LEE: Then it's a date.

SAUL: Well, I'll call the country club and see if I can arrange something.

LEE: Great! Boy, I sure am sorry that I busted in on ya' all in the middle of yer meeting.

SAUL: Oh that's quite all right. We were just about finished anyway.

LEE: I can wait out in the other room if you want.

SAUL: No really—

LEE: Just got Austin's color TV back from the shop. I can watch a little amateur boxing now.

(LEE *and* AUSTIN *exchange looks.*)

SAUL: Oh— Yes.

LEE: You don't fool around in Television, do you Saul?

SAUL: Uh— I have in the past. Produced some TV Specials.

21

Network stuff. But it's mainly features now.

LEE: That's where the big money is, huh?

SAUL: Yes. That's right.

AUSTIN: Why don't I call you tomorrow, Saul, and we'll get together. We can have lunch or something.

SAUL: That'd be terrific.

LEE: Right after the golf.

(*Pause*)

SAUL: What?

LEE: You can have lunch right after the golf.

SAUL: Oh, right.

LEE: Austin was tellin' me that yer interested in stories.

SAUL: Well, we develop certain projects that we feel have commercial potential.

LEE: What kinda' stuff do ya' go in for?

SAUL: Oh, the usual. You know. Good love interest. Lots of action. (*Chuckles at* AUSTIN.)

LEE: Westerns?

SAUL: Sometimes.

AUSTIN: I'll give you a ring, Saul.

(AUSTIN *tries to move* SAUL *across the kitchen but* LEE *blocks their way.*)

LEE: I got a Western that'd knock yer lights out.

SAUL: Oh really?

LEE: Yeah. Contemporary Western. Based on a true story. 'Course I'm not a writer like my brother here. I'm not a man of the pen.

SAUL: Well—

LEE: I mean I can tell ya' a story off the tongue but I can't put it down on paper. That don't make any difference though does it?

SAUL: No, not really.

LEE: I mean plenty a' guys have stories don't they? True-life stories. Musta' been a lota' movies made from real life.

SAUL: Yes. I suppose so.

LEE: I haven't seen a good Western since *Lonely are the Brave.* You remember that movie?

SAUL: No, I'm afraid I—

22

LEE: Kirk Douglas. Helluva' movie. You remember that movie, Austin?

AUSTIN: Yes.

LEE: (*To* SAUL) The man dies for the love of a horse.

SAUL: Is that right.

LEE: Yeah. Ya' hear the horse screamin' at the end of it. Rain's comin' down. Horse is screamin'. Then there's a shot. BLAM! Just a single shot like that. Then nothin' but the sound of rain. And Kirk Douglas is ridin' in the ambulance. Ridin' away from the scene of the accident. And when he hears that shot he knows that his horse has died. He knows. And you see his eyes. And his eyes die. Right inside his face. And then his eyes close. And you know that he's died too. You know that Kirk Douglas has died from the death of his horse.

SAUL: (*Eyes* AUSTIN *nervously*) Well, it sounds like a great movie. I'm sorry I missed it.

LEE: Yeah, you shouldn't a' missed that one.

SAUL: I'll have to try to catch it some time. Arrange a screening or something. Well, Austin, I'll have to hit the freeway before rush hour.

AUSTIN: (*Ushers* SAUL *toward exit*) It's good seeing you, Saul. (AUSTIN *and* SAUL *shake hands.*)

LEE: So ya' think there's room for a real Western these days? A true-to-life Western?

SAUL: Well, I don't see why not. Why don't you uh—tell the story to Austin and have him write a little outline.

LEE: You'd take a look at it then?

SAUL: Yes. Sure. I'll give it a read-through. Always eager for new material. (*Smiles at* AUSTIN.)

LEE: That's great! You'd really read it then, huh?

SAUL: It would just be my opinion of course.

LEE: That's all I want. Just an opinion. I happen to think it has a lota' possibilities.

SAUL: Well, it was great meeting you and I'll— (SAUL *and* LEE *shake.*)

LEE: I'll call you tomorrow about the golf.

SAUL: Oh. Yes, right.

LEE: Austin's got your number, right?

SAUL: Yes.

LEE: So long, Saul.

> (LEE *gives* SAUL *a pat on the back.* SAUL *exits,* AUSTIN *turns to* LEE, *looks at TV, then back to* LEE.)

AUSTIN: Give me the keys.

> (AUSTIN *extends his hand toward* LEE, LEE *doesn't move, just stares at* AUSTIN, *smiles. Lights to black.*)

SCENE FOUR

Night, coyotes in distance, fade, sound of typewriter in dark, crickets, candlelight in alcove, dim light in kitchen. Lights reveal AUSTIN *at glass table typing,* LEE *sits across from him, foot on table, drinking beer and whiskey; the TV is still on sink counter,* AUSTIN *types for a while then stops.*

LEE: All right, now read it back to me.

AUSTIN: I'm not reading it back to you, Lee. You can read it when we're finished. I can't spend all night on this.

LEE: You got better things to do?

AUSTIN: Let's just go ahead. Now what happens when he leaves Texas?

LEE: Is he ready to leave Texas yet? I didn't know we were that far along. He's not ready to leave Texas.

AUSTIN: He's right at the border.

LEE: (*Sitting up*) No, see, this is one a' the crucial parts. Right here. (*Taps paper with beer can.*) We can't rush through this. He's not right at the border. He's a good fifty miles from the border. A lot can happen in fifty miles.

AUSTIN: It's only an outline. We're not writing an entire script now.

LEE: Well ya' can't leave things out even if it is an outline. It's one a' the most important parts. Ya' can't go leavin' it out.

AUSTIN: Okay, okay. Let's just—get it done.

LEE: All right. Now. He's in the truck and he's got his horse trailer and his horse.

AUSTIN: We've already established that.

LEE: And he sees this other guy comin' up behind him in another truck. And that truck is pullin' a gooseneck.

AUSTIN: What's a gooseneck?

LEE: Cattle trailer. You know the kind with a gooseneck, goes right down in the bed a' the pick-up.

AUSTIN: Oh. All right. (*Types*)

LEE: It's important.

AUSTIN: Okay. I got it.

LEE: All these details are important.

(AUSTIN *types as they talk.*)

AUSTIN: I've got it.

LEE: And this other guy's got his horse all saddled up in the back a' the gooseneck.

AUSTIN: Right.

LEE: So both these guys have got their horses right along with 'em, see.

AUSTIN: I understand.

LEE: Then this first guy suddenly realizes two things.

AUSTIN: The guy in front?

LEE: Right. The guy in front realizes two things almost at the same time. Simultaneous.

AUSTIN: What were the two things?

LEE: Number one, he realizes that the guy behind him is the husband of the woman he's been— (LEE *makes gesture of screwing by pumping his arm.*)

AUSTIN: (*Sees* LEE's *gesture*) Oh. Yeah.

LEE: And number two, he realizes he's in the middle of Tornado Country.

AUSTIN: What's 'Tornado Country'?

LEE: Panhandle.

AUSTIN: Panhandle?

LEE: Sweetwater. Around in that area. Nothin'. Nowhere. And number three—

AUSTIN: I thought there was only two.

LEE: There's three. There's a third unforeseen realization.

AUSTIN: And what's that?

LEE: That he's runnin' outa' gas.

AUSTIN: (*Stops typing*) Come on, Lee. (*He gets up, moves to kitchen, gets a glass of water.*)

LEE: Whadya' mean, 'come on'? That's what it is. Write it down! He's runnin' outa' gas.

AUSTIN: It's too—

LEE: What? It's too what? It's too real! That's what ya' mean isn't it? It's too much like real life!

AUSTIN: It's not like real life! It's not enough like real life. Things don't happen like that.

LEE: What! Men don't fuck other men's women?

AUSTIN: Yes. But they don't end up chasing each other across the Panhandle. Through 'Tornado Country'.

LEE: They do in this movie!

AUSTIN: And they don't have horses conveniently along with them when they run out of gas! And they don't run out of gas either!

LEE: These guys run outa' gas! This is my story and one a' these guys runs outa' gas!

AUSTIN: It's just a dumb excuse to get them into a chase scene. It's contrived.

LEE: It is a chase scene! It's already a chase scene. They been chasin' each other fer days.

AUSTIN: So now they're supposed to abandon their trucks, climb on their horses and chase each other into the mountains?

LEE: (*Standing suddenly*) There aren't any mountains in the Panhandle! It's flat!! (*He turns violently toward windows in alcove and throws beer can at them.*) Goddamn these crickets! (*Yells at crickets.*) Shut up out there! (*Pause, turns back toward table.*) This place is like a fuckin' rest home here. How're you supposed to think!

AUSTIN: You wanna' take a break?

LEE: No, I don't wanna' take a break! I wanna' get this done! This is my last chance to get this done.

AUSTIN: (*Moves back into alcove*) All right. Take it easy.

LEE: I'm gonna' be leavin' this area. I don't have time to mess around here.

AUSTIN: Where are you going?

LEE: Never mind where I'm goin'! That's got nothin' to do with

you. I just gotta' get this done. I'm not like you. Hangin'
around bein' a parasite offa' other fools. I gotta' do this
thing and get out.

(*Pause*)

AUSTIN: A parasite? Me?

LEE: Yeah, you!

AUSTIN: After you break into people's houses and take their
televisions?

LEE: They don't need their televisions! I'm doin' them a service.

AUSTIN: Give me back my keys, Lee.

LEE: Not until you write this thing! You're gonna' write this
outline thing for me or that car's gonna wind up in Arizona
with a different paint job.

AUSTIN: You think you can force me to write this? I was doing
you a favor.

LEE: Git off yer high horse will ya'! Favor! Big favor. Handin'
down favors from the mountain top.

AUSTIN: Let's just write it, okay? Let's sit down and not get upset
and see if we can just get through this.

(AUSTIN *sits at typewriter. Long pause.*)

LEE: Yer not gonna' even show it to him, are ya'?

AUSTIN: What?

LEE: This outline. You got no intention of showin' it to him. Yer
just doin' this 'cause yer afraid a' me.

AUSTIN: You can show it to him yourself.

LEE: I will, boy! I'm gonna' read it to him on the golf course.

AUSTIN: And I'm not afraid of you either.

LEE: Then how come yer doin' it?

AUSTIN: (*Pause*) So I can get my keys back.

(*Pause as* LEE *takes keys out of his pocket slowly and throws
them on table. Long pause.* AUSTIN *stares at keys.*)

LEE: There. Now you got yer keys back.

(AUSTIN *looks up at* LEE *but doesn't take keys.*)

Go ahead. There's yer keys.

(AUSTIN *slowly takes keys off table and puts them back in his
own pocket.*)

Now what're you gonna' do? Kick me out?

AUSTIN: I'm not going to kick you out, Lee.

27

LEE: You couldn't kick me out, boy.

AUSTIN: I know.

LEE: So you can't even consider that one. (*Pause*) You could call the Police. That'd be the obvious thing.

AUSTIN: You're my brother.

LEE: That don't mean a thing. You go down to the L.A. Police Department there and ask them what kinda' people kill each other most. What do you think they'd say?

AUSTIN: Who said anything about killing?

LEE: Family people. Brothers. Brothers-in-Law. Cousins. Real American-type people. They kill each other in the heat mostly. In the Smog-Alerts. In the Brush-Fire Season. Right about this time a' year.

AUSTIN: This isn't the same.

LEE: Oh no? What makes it different?

AUSTIN: We're not insane. We're not driven to acts of violence like that. Not over a dumb movie script. Now sit down.
(*Long pause,* LEE *considers which way to go with it.*)

LEE: Maybe not. (*He sits back down at table across from* AUSTIN.) Maybe you're right. Maybe we're too intelligent, huh? (*Pause*) We got our heads on our shoulders. One of us has even got a Ivy League diploma. Now that means somethin' don't it? Doesn't that mean somethin'?

AUSTIN: Look, I'll write this thing for you, Lee. I don't mind writing it. I just don't want to get all worked up about it. It's not worth it. Now, come on. Let's just get through it, okay?

LEE: Nah. I think there's easier money. Lotsa' places I could pick up thousands. Maybe millions. I don't need this shit. I could go up to Sacramento Valley and steal me a diesel. Ten thousand a week dismantling one a' those suckers. Ten thousand a week! (*He opens another beer, puts his foot back up on table.*)

AUSTIN: No, really, look, I'll write it out for you. I think it's a great idea.

LEE: Nah, you got yer own work to do. I don't wanna' interfere with yer life.

AUSTIN: I mean it'd be really fantastic if you could sell this. Turn

28

it into a movie. I mean it.

(*Pause*)

LEE: Ya' think so, huh?

AUSTIN: Absolutely. You could really turn your life around, you know. Change things.

LEE: I could get me a house maybe.

AUSTIN: Sure you could get a house. You could get a whole ranch if you wanted to.

LEE: (*Laughs*) A ranch? I could get a ranch?

AUSTIN: 'Course you could. You know what a screenplay sells for these days?

LEE: No. What's it sell for?

AUSTIN: A lot. A whole lot of money.

LEE: Thousands?

AUSTIN: Yeah. Thousands.

LEE: Millions?

AUSTIN: Well—

LEE: We could get the old man outa' hock then.

AUSTIN: Maybe.

LEE: Maybe? Whadya' mean, maybe?

AUSTIN: I mean it might take more than money.

LEE: You were just tellin' me it'd change my whole life around. Why wouldn't it change his?

AUSTIN: He's different.

LEE: Oh, he's of a different ilk, huh?

AUSTIN: He's not gonna' change. Let's leave the old man out of it.

LEE: That's right. He's not gonna' change but I will. I'll just turn myself right inside out. I could be just like you then, huh? Sittin' around dreamin' stuff up. Gettin' paid to dream. Ridin' back and forth on the freeway just dreamin' my fool head off.

AUSTIN: It's not all that easy.

LEE: It's not, huh?

AUSTIN: No. There's a lot of work involved.

LEE: What's the toughest part? Deciding whether to jog or play tennis?

(*Long pause.*)

AUSTIN: Well, look. You can stay here—do whatever you want to. Borrow the car. Come in and out. Doesn't matter to me. It's not my house. I'll help you write this thing or—not. Just let me know what you want. You tell me.

LEE: Oh. So now suddenly you're at my service. Is that it?

AUSTIN: What do you want to do, Lee?

(*Long pause.* LEE *stares at him then turns and dreams at windows.*)

LEE: I tell ya' what I'd do if I still had that dog. Ya' wanna' know what I'd do?

AUSTIN: What?

LEE: Head out to Ventura. Cook up a little match. God that little dog could bear down. Lota' money in dog fightin'. Big money.

(*Pause*)

AUSTIN: Why don't we try to see this through, Lee. Just for the hell of it. Maybe you've really got something here. What do you think?

(*Pause.* LEE *considers.*)

LEE: Maybe so. No harm in tryin' I guess. You think it's such a hot idea. Besides, I always wondered what'd be like to be you.

AUSTIN: You did?

LEE: Yeah, sure. I used to picture you walkin' around some campus with yer arms fulla' books. Blondes chasin' after ya'.

AUSTIN: Blondes? That's funny.

LEE: What's funny about it?

AUSTIN: Because I always used to picture you somewhere.

LEE: Where'd you picture me?

AUSTIN: Oh, I don't know. Different places. Adventures. You were always on some adventure.

LEE: Yeah.

AUSTIN: And I used to say to myself, 'Lee's got the right idea. He's out there in the world and here I am. What am I doing?'

LEE: Well you were settin' yourself up for somethin'.

AUSTIN: I guess.

LEE: We better get started on this thing then.

30

AUSTIN: Okay. (*He sits up at typewriter, puts new paper in.*)
LEE: Oh. Can I get the keys back before I forget?
(AUSTIN *hesitates.*)
You said I could borrow the car if I wanted, right? Isn't that what you said?
AUSTIN: Yeah. Right.
(AUSTIN *takes keys out of his pocket, sets them on table,* LEE *takes keys slowly, plays with them in his hand.*)
LEE: I could get a ranch, huh?
AUSTIN: Yeah. We have to write it first though.
LEE: Okay. Let's write it.
(*Lights start dimming slowly to end of scene as* AUSTIN *types,* LEE *speaks.*)
So they take off after each other straight into an endless black prairie. The sun is just comin' down and they can feel the night on their backs. What they don't know is that each one of 'em is afraid see. Each one separately thinks that he's the only one that's afraid. And they keep ridin' like that straight into the night. Not knowing. And the one who's chasin' doesn't know where the other one is taking him. And the one who's being chased doesn't know where he's going.
(*Lights to black, typing stops in the dark, crickets fade. Music in Act break: Hank Williams' 'Ramblin' Man'.*)

ACT TWO

SCENE FIVE

Morning, LEE *at table in alcove with a set of golf clubs in a fancy leather bag,* AUSTIN *at sink washing a few dishes.*

AUSTIN: He really liked it, huh?

LEE: He wouldn't a' gave me these clubs if he didn't like it.

AUSTIN: He gave you the clubs?

LEE: Yeah. I told ya' he gave me the clubs. The bag too.

AUSTIN: I thought he just loaned them to you.

LEE: He said it was part a' the advance. A little gift like. Gesture of his good faith.

AUSTIN: He's giving you an advance?

LEE: Now what's so amazing about that? I told ya' it was a good story. You even said it was a good story.

AUSTIN: Well that is really incredible, Lee. You know how many guys spend their whole lives down here trying to break into this business? Just trying to get in the door?

LEE: (*Pulling clubs out of bag, testing them*) I got no idea. How many?

(*Pause*)

AUSTIN: How much of an advance is he giving you?

LEE: Plenty. We were talkin' big money out there. Ninth hole is where I sealed the deal.

AUSTIN: He made a firm commitment?

LEE: Absolutely.

AUSTIN: Well, I know Saul and he doesn't fool around when he says he likes something.

LEE: I thought you said you didn't know him.

AUSTIN: Well, I'm familiar with his tastes.

LEE: I let him get two up on me goin' into the back nine. He was sure he had me cold. You shoulda' seen his face when I pulled out the old pitching wedge and plopped it pin-high,

32

two feet from the cup. He 'bout shit his pants. 'Where'd a guy like you ever learn how to play golf like that?' he says.

(LEE *laughs*, AUSTIN *stares at him.*)

AUSTIN: 'Course there's no contract yet. Nothing's final until it's on paper.

LEE: It's final, all right. There's no way he's gonna' back out of it now. We gambled for it.

AUSTIN: Saul, gambled?

LEE: Yeah, sure. I mean he liked the outline already so he wasn't risking that much. I just guaranteed it with my short game. (*Pause*)

AUSTIN: Well, we should celebrate or something. If think Mom left a bottle of Champagne in the refrigerator. We should have a little toast.

(AUSTIN *gets glasses from cupboard, goes to refrigerator, pulls out bottle of Champagne.*)

LEE: You shouldn't oughta' take her Champagne, Austin. She's gonna' miss that.

AUSTIN: Oh, she's not going to mind. She'd be glad we put it to good use. I'll get her another bottle. Besides, it's perfect for the occasion.

(*Pause*)

LEE: Yer gonna' get a nice fee fer writin' the script a' course. Straight fee.

(AUSTIN *stops, stares at* LEE, *puts glasses and bottle on table. Pause*)

AUSTIN: I'm writing the script?

LEE: That's what he said. Said we couldn't hire a better screenwriter in the whole town.

AUSTIN: But I'm already working on a script. I've got my own project. I don't have time to write two scripts.

LEE: No, he said he was gonna' drop that other one. (*Pause*)

AUSTIN: What? You mean mine? He's going to drop mine and do yours instead?

LEE: (*Smiles*) Now look, Austin, it's jest beginner's luck ya' know. I mean I sank a fifty-foot putt for this deal. No hard feelings.

C   33

(AUSTIN *goes to phone on wall, grabs it, starts dialing.*)
He's not gonna' be in, Austin. Told me he wouldn't be in
'til late this afternoon.

AUSTIN: (*Stays on phone, dialing, listens*) I can't believe this. I just
can't believe it. Are you sure he said that? Why would he
drop mine?

LEE: That's what he told me.

AUSTIN: He can't do that without telling me first. Without talking
to me at least. He wouldn't just make a decision like that
without talking to me!

LEE: Well I was kinda' surprised myself. But he was real
enthusiastic about my story.

(AUSTIN *hangs up phone violently, paces.*)

AUSTIN: What'd he say! Tell me everything he said!

LEE: I been tellin' ya'! He said he liked the story a whole lot. It
was the first authentic Western to come along in a decade.

AUSTIN: He liked that story? Your story?

LEE: Yeah! What's so surprisin' about that?

AUSTIN: It's stupid! It's the dumbest story I ever heard in my life.

LEE: Hey, hold on! That's my story yer talkin' about!

AUSTIN: It's a bullshit story! It's idiotic. Two lamebrains chasing
each other across Texas! Are you kidding? Who do you
think's going to go see a film like that?

LEE: It's not a film! It's a movie. There's a big difference. That's
somethin' Saul told me.

AUSTIN: Oh he did, huh?

LEE: Yeah, he said, 'In this business we make Movies, American
Movies. Leave the Films to the French.'

AUSTIN: So you got real intimate with old Saul, huh? He started
pouring forth his vast knowledge of Cinema.

LEE: I think he liked me a lot, to tell ya' the truth. I think he felt
I was somebody he could confide in.

AUSTIN: What'd you do, beat him up or something?

LEE: (*Stands fast*) Hey, I've about had it with the insults, buddy!
You think yer the only one in the brain department here? Yer
the only one that can sit around and cook things up? There's
other people got ideas too, ya' know!

AUSTIN: You must've done something. Threatened him or

34

something. Now what'd you do, Lee?

LEE: I convinced him!

(LEE *makes sudden menacing lunge toward* AUSTIN, *weilding golf club above his head, stops himself, frozen moment, long pause.* LEE *lowers club.*)

AUSTIN: Oh, Jesus. You didn't hurt him did you?

(*Long silence,* LEE *sits back down at table.*)

Lee! Did you hurt him?

LEE: I didn't do nothin' to him! He liked my story. Pure and simple. He said it was the best story he's come across in a long, long time.

AUSTIN: That's what he told me about my story! That's the same thing he said to me.

LEE: Well, he musta' been lyin'. He musta' been lyin' to one of us anyway.

AUSTIN: You can't come into this town and start pushing people around. They're gonna' put you away!

LEE: I never pushed anybody around! I beat him fair and square. (*Pause*) They can't touch me anyway. They can't put a finger on me. I'm gone. I can come in through the window and go out through the door. They never knew what hit 'em. You, yer stuck. Yer the one that's stuck. Not me. So don't be warnin' me what to do in this town.

(*Pause,* AUSTIN *crosses to table, sits at typewriter, rest.*)

AUSTIN: Lee come, on, level with me will you? It doesn't make any sense that suddenly he'd throw my idea out the window. I've been talking to him for months. I've got too much at stake. Everything's riding on this project.

LEE: What's yer idea?

AUSTIN: It's just a simple love story.

LEE: What kinda' love story?

AUSTIN: (*Stands, crosses into kitchen*) I'm not telling you!

LEE: Ha! 'Fraid I'll steal it, huh? Competition's gettin' kinda' close to home isn't it?

AUSTIN: Where did Saul say he was going?

LEE: He was gonna' take my story to a couple studios.

AUSTIN: That's *my* outline you know! I wrote that outline! You've got no right to be peddling it around.

LEE: You weren't ready to take credit for it last night.

AUSTIN: Give me my keys!

LEE: What?

AUSTIN: The keys! I want my keys back!

LEE: Where you goin'?

AUSTIN: Just give me my keys! I gotta' take a drive. I gotta' get out of here for a while.

LEE: Where you gonna' go, Austin?

AUSTIN: (*Pause*) I might just drive out to the desert for a while. I gotta' think.

LEE: You can think here just as good. This is the perfect set-up for thinkin'. We got some writin' to do here, boy. Now let's just have us a little toast. Relax. We're partners now.
(LEE *pops the cork of the Champagne bottle, pours two drinks as the lights fade to black.*)

SCENE SIX

Afternoon, LEE *and* SAUL *in kitchen,* AUSTIN *in alcove.*

LEE: Now you tell him. You tell him, Mr Kipper.

SAUL: Kimmer.

LEE: Kimmer. You tell him what you told me. He don't believe me.

AUSTIN: I don't want to hear it.

SAUL: It's really not a big issue. Austin. I was simply amazed by your brother's story and—

AUSTIN: Amazed? You lost a bet! You gambled with my material!

SAUL: That's really beside the point, Austin. I'm ready to go all the way with your brother's story. I think it has a great deal of merit.

AUSTIN: I don't want to hear about it, okay? Go tell it to the executives! Tell it to somebody who's going to turn it into a package deal or something. A TV series. Don't tell it to me.

SAUL: But I want to continue with your project too, Austin. It's not as though we can't do both. We're big enough for that aren't we?

36

AUSTIN: 'We'? *I* can't do both! I don't know about 'we'.

LEE: (*To* SAUL) See, what'd I tell ya'. He's totally unsympathetic.

SAUL: Austin, there's no point in our going to another screenwriter for this. It just doesn't make sense. You're brothers. You know each other. There's a familiarity with material that just wouldn't be possible otherwise.

AUSTIN: There's no familiarity with the material! None! I don't know what 'Tornado Country' is. I don't know what a 'gooseneck' is. And I don't want to know! (*Pointing to* LEE.) He's a hustler! He's a bigger hustler than you are! If you can't see that, then—

LEE: (*To* AUSTIN) Hey, now hold on. I didn't have to bring this bone back to you, boy. I persuaded Saul here that you were the right man for the job. You don't have to go throwin' up favors in my face.

AUSTIN: Favors! I'm the one who wrote the fuckin' outline! You can't even spell.

SAUL: (*To* AUSTIN) Your brother told me about the situation with your father.

(*Pause*)

AUSTIN: What? (*Looks at* LEE.)

SAUL: That's right. Now we have a clear cut deal here, Austin. We have big studio money standing behind this thing. Just on the basis of your outline.

AUSTIN: (*To* SAUL) What'd he tell you about my father?

SAUL: Well—that he's destitute. He needs money.

LEE: That's right. He does.

(AUSTIN *shakes his head, stares at them both.*)

AUSTIN: (*To* LEE) And this little assignment is supposed to go toward the old man? A charity project? Is that what this is? Did you cook this up on the ninth green too?

SAUL: It's a big slice, Austin.

AUSTIN: (*To* LEE) I gave him money! I already gave him money. You know that. He drank it all up!

LEE: This is a different deal here.

SAUL: We can set up a trust for your father. A large sum of money. It can be doled out to him in parcels so he can't misuse it.

37

AUSTIN: Yeah, and who's doing the doling?

SAUL: Your brother volunteered.

(AUSTIN *laughs*.)

LEE: That's right. I'll make sure he uses it for groceries.

AUSTIN: (*To* SAUL) I'm not doing this script! I'm not writing this crap for you or anybody else. You can't blackmail me into it. You can't threaten me into it. There's no way I'm doing it. So just give it up. Both of you.

(*Long pause*.)

SAUL: Well, that's it then. I mean this is an easy three hundred grand. Just for a first draft. It's incredible, Austin. We've got three different studios all trying to cut each other's throats to get this material. In one morning. That's how hot it is.

AUSTIN: Yeah, well you can afford to give me a percentage on the outline then. And you better get the genius here an agent before he gets burned.

LEE: Saul's gonna' be my agent. Isn't that right, Saul?

SAUL: That's right. (*To* AUSTIN.) Your brother has really got something, Austin. I've been around too long not to recognize it. Raw talent.

AUSTIN: He's got a lota' balls is what he's got. He's taking you right down the river.

SAUL: Three hundred thousand, Austin. Just for a first draft. Now you've never been offered that kind of money before.

AUSTIN: I'm not writing it.

(*Pause*)

SAUL: I see. Well—

LEE: We'll just go to another writer then. Right, Saul? Just hire us somebody with some enthusiasm. Somebody who can recognize the value of a good story.

SAUL: I'm sorry about this, Austin.

AUSTIN: Yeah.

SAUL: I mean I was hoping we could continue both things but now I don't see how it's possible.

AUSTIN: So you're dropping my idea altogether. Is that it? Just trade horses in mid-stream? After all these months of meetings.

38

SAUL: I wish there was another way.

AUSTIN: I've got everything riding on this, Saul. You know that. It's my only shot. If this falls through—

SAUL: I have to go with what my instincts tell me—

AUSTIN: Your instincts!

SAUL: My gut reaction.

AUSTIN: You lost! That's your gut reaction. You lost a gamble. Now you're trying to tell me you like his story? How could you possibly fall for that story? It's as phony as Hopalong Cassidy. What do you see in it? I'm curious.

SAUL: It has the ring of truth, Austin.

AUSTIN: (*Laughs*) Truth?

LEE: It is true.

SAUL: Something about the real West.

AUSTIN: Why? Because it's got horses? Because it's got grown men acting like little boys?

SAUL: Something about the land. Your brother is speaking from experience.

AUSTIN: So am I!

SAUL: But nobody's interested in love these days, Austin. Let's face it.

LEE: That's right.

AUSTIN: (*To* SAUL) He's been camped out on the desert for three months. Talking to cactus. What's he know about what people wanna' see on the screen! I drive on the freeway every day. I swallow the smog. I watch the news in color. I shop in the Safeway. I'm the one who's in touch! Not him!

SAUL: I have to go now, Austin. (*He starts to leave.*)

AUSTIN: There's no such thing as the West anymore! It's a dead issue! It's dried up, Saul, and so are you.

(SAUL *stops and turns to* AUSTIN.)

SAUL: Maybe you're right. But I have to take the gamble, don't I?

AUSTIN: You're a fool to do this, Saul.

SAUL: I've always gone on my hunches. Always. And I've never been wrong. (*To* LEE.) I'll talk to you tomorrow, Lee.

LEE: All right, Mr Kimmer.

SAUL: Maybe we could have some lunch.

39

LEE: Fine with me. (*Smiles at* AUSTIN.)

SAUL: I'll give you a ring.

(SAUL *exits, lights to black as brothers look at each other from a distance.*)

SCENE SEVEN

Night, coyotes, crickets, sound of typewriter in dark, candlelight up on LEE *at typewriter struggling to type with one-finger system,* AUSTIN *sits sprawled out on kitchen floor with whiskey bottle, drunk.*

AUSTIN: (*Singing, from floor*)

Red sails in the sunset
Way out on the blue
Please carry my loved one
Home safely to me

Red sails in the sunset—

LEE: (*Slams fist on table*) Hey! Knock it off will ya'! I'm tryin' to concentrate here.

AUSTIN: (*Laughs*) You're tryin' to concentrate?

LEE: Yeah. That's right.

AUSTIN: Now you're tryin' to concentrate.

LEE: Between you, the coyotes and the crickets a thought don't have much of a chance.

AUSTIN: 'Between me, the coyotes and the crickets.' What a great title.

LEE: I don't need a title! I need a thought.

AUSTIN: (*Laughs*) A thought! Here's a thought for ya'—

LEE: I'm not askin' fer yer thoughts! I got my own. I can do this thing on my own.

AUSTIN: You're going to write an entire script on your own?

LEE: That's right.

(*Pause*)

AUSTIN: Here's a thought. Saul Kimmer—

LEE: Shut up will ya'!

AUSTIN: He thinks we're the same person.

40

LEE: Don't get cute.

AUSTIN: He does! He's lost his mind. Poor old Saul. (*Giggles*)
     Thinks we're one and the same.

LEE: Why don't you ease up on that Champagne.

AUSTIN: (*Holding up bottle*) This isn't Champagne anymore. We
     went through the Champagne a long time ago. This is
     serious stuff. The days of Champagne are long gone.

LEE: Well go outside and drink it.

AUSTIN: I'm enjoying your company, Lee. For the first time since
     your arrival I am finally enjoying your company. And now
     you want me to go outside and drink alone?

LEE: That's right. (*He reads through paper in typewriter, makes an
     erasure.*)

AUSTIN: You think you'll make more progress if you're alone?
     You might drive yourself crazy.

LEE: I could have this thing done in a night if I had a little
     silence.

AUSTIN: Well you'd still have the crickets to contend with. The
     coyotes. The sounds of the Police Helicopters prowling
     above the neighborhood. Slashing their searchlights down
     through the streets. Hunting for the likes of you.

LEE: I'm a screenwriter now! I'm legitimate.

AUSTIN: (*Laughing*) A screenwriter!

LEE: That's right. I'm on salary. That's more'n I can say for you.
     I got an advance coming.

AUSTIN: This is true. This is very true. An advance. (*Pause*) Well,
     maybe I oughta' go out and try my hand at your trade.
     Since you're doing so good at mine.

LEE: Ha! (*He attempts to type some more but gets the ribbon
     tangled up, starts trying to rethread it as they continue talking.*)

AUSTIN: Well why not? You don't think I've got what it takes to
     sneak into people's houses and steal their TVs?

LEE: You couldn't steal a toaster without losin' yer lunch.
     (AUSTIN *stands with a struggle, supports himself by the sink.*)

AUSTIN: You don't think I could sneak into somebody's house
     and steal a toaster?

LEE: Go take a shower or somethin' will ya! (*He gets more tangled
     up with the typewriter ribbon, pulling it out of the machine as*

41

though it was fishing line.)

AUSTIN: You really don't think I could steal a crumby toaster? How much you wanna' bet I can't steal a toaster! How much? Go ahead! You're a gambler aren't you? Tell me how much yer willing to put on the line. Some part of your big advance? Oh, you haven't got that yet have you. I forgot.

LEE: All right. I'll bet you your car that you can't steal a toaster without gettin' busted.

AUSTIN: You already got my car!

LEE: Okay, your house then.

AUSTIN: What're you gonna' give me! I'm not talkin' about my house and my car, I'm talkin' about what are you gonna' give me. You don't have nothin' to give me.

LEE: I'll give you—shared screen credit. How 'bout that? I'll have it put in the contract that this was written by the both of us.

AUSTIN: I don't want my name on that piece of shit! I want something of value. You got anything of value? You got any tidbits from the desert? Any Rattlesnake bones? I'm not a greedy man. Any little personal treasure will suffice.

LEE: I'm gonna' just kick yer ass out in a minute.

AUSTIN: Oh, so now you're gonna' kick me out! Now I'm the intruder. I'm the one who's invading your precious privacy.

LEE: I'm trying to do some screenwriting here! (*He stands, picks up typewriter, slams it down hard on table. Pause, silence except for crickets.*)

AUSTIN: Well, you got everything you need. You got plenty a' coffee? Groceries. You got a car. A contract. (*Pause*) Might need a new typewriter ribbon but other than that you're pretty well fixed. I'll just leave ya' alone for a while. (*AUSTIN tries to steady himself to leave, LEE makes a move toward him.*)

LEE: Where you goin'?

AUSTIN: Don't worry about me. I'm not the one to worry about. (*He weaves toward exit, stops.*)

LEE: What're you gonna' do? Just go wander out into the night?

AUSTIN: I'm gonna' make a little tour.

LEE: Why don't ya' just go to bed for Christ's sake. Yer makin'

42

me sick.

AUSTIN: I can take care a' myself. Don't worry about me.
(AUSTIN *weaves badly in another attempt to exit, he crashes to the floor,* LEE *goes to him but remains standing.*)

LEE: You want me to call your wife for ya' or something?

AUSTIN: (*From floor*) My wife?

LEE: Yeah. I mean maybe she can help ya' out. Talk to ya' or somethin'.

AUSTIN: (*Struggles to stand up again*) She's five hundred miles away. North. North of here. Up in the north country where things are calm. I don't need any help. I'm gonna' go outside and I'm gonna' steal a toaster. I'm gonna' steal some other stuff too. I might even commit bigger crimes. Bigger than you ever dreamed of. Crimes beyond the imagination!
(AUSTIN *manages to get himself vertical, tries to head for exit again.*)

LEE: Just hang on a minute, Austin.

AUSTIN: Why? What for? You don't need my help, right? You got a handle on the project. Besides, I'm lookin' forward to the smell of the night. The bushes. Orange blossoms. Dust in the driveways. Rain bird sprinklers. Lights in people's houses. You're right about the lights, Lee. Everybody else is livin' the life. Indoors. Safe. This is a Paradise down here. You know that? We're livin' in a Paradise. We've forgotten about that.

LEE: You sound just like the old man now.

AUSTIN: Yeah, well we all sound alike when we're sloshed. We just sorta' echo each other.

LEE: Maybe if we could work on this together we could bring him back out here. Get him settled down some place.
(AUSTIN *turns violently toward* LEE, *takes a swing at him, misses and crashes to the floor again.* LEE *stays standing.*)

AUSTIN: I don't want him out here! I've had it with him! I went all the way out there! I went out of my way. I gave him money and all he did was play Al Jolson records and spit at me! I gave him money!
(*Pause*)

LEE: Just help me a little with the characters, all right? You know

43

how to do it, Austin.

AUSTIN: (*On floor, laughs*) The characters!

LEE: Yeah. You know. The way they talk and stuff. I can hear it in my head but I can't get it down on paper.

AUSTIN: What characters?

LEE: The guys. The guys in the story.

AUSTIN: Those aren't characters.

LEE: Whatever you call 'em then. I need to write somethin' out.

AUSTIN: Those are illusions of characters.

LEE: I don't give a damn what ya' call 'em! You know what I'm talkin' about!

AUSTIN: Those are fantasies of a long lost boyhood.

LEE: I gotta' write somethin' out on paper!
(*Pause*)

AUSTIN: What for? Saul's gonna' get you a fancy screenwriter isn't he?

LEE: I wanna' do it myself!

AUSTIN: Then do it! Yer on your own now old buddy. You bulldogged yer way into contention. Now you gotta' carry it through.

LEE: I will but I need some advice. Just a couple a' things. Come on, Austin. Just help me get 'em talkin' right. It won't take much.

AUSTIN: Oh, now you're having a little doubt, huh? What happened? The pressure's on, boy. This is it. You gotta' come up with it now. You don't come up with a winner on your first time out they just cut your head off. They don't give you a second chance ya' know.

LEE: I got a good story! I know it's a good story. I just need a little help is all.

AUSTIN: Not from me. Not from yer little old brother. I'm retired.

LEE: You could save this thing for me, Austin. I'd give ya' half the money. I would. I only need half anyway. With this kinda' money I could be a long time down the road. I'd never bother ya' again. I promise. You'd never even see me again.

AUSTIN: (*Still on floor*) You'd disappear?

LEE: I would for sure.

AUSTIN: Where would you disappear to?

LEE: That don't matter. I got plenty a' places.

AUSTIN: Nobody can disappear. The old man tried that. Look where it got him. He lost his teeth.

LEE: He never had any money.

AUSTIN: I don't mean that. I mean his teeth! His real teeth. First he lost his real teeth, then he lost his false teeth. You never knew that did ya'? He never confided in you.

LEE: Nah, I never knew that.

AUSTIN: You wanna' drink?

(AUSTIN *offers bottle to* LEE, LEE *takes it, sits down on kitchen floor with* AUSTIN, *they share the bottle.*)

Yeah, he lost his real teeth one at a time. Woke up every morning with another tooth lying on the mattress. Finally, he decides he's gotta' get 'em all pulled out but he doesn't have any money. Middle of Arizona with no money and no insurance and every morning another tooth is lying on the mattress. (*Takes a drink.*) So what does he do?

LEE: I dunno'. I never knew about that.

AUSTIN: He begs the government. GI Bill or some damn thing. Some pension plan he remembers in the back of his head. And they send him out the money.

LEE: They did?

(*They keep trading the bottle between them, taking drinks.*)

AUSTIN: Yeah. They send him the money but it's not enough money. Costs a lot to have all yer teeth yanked. They charge by the individual tooth, ya' know. I mean one tooth isn't equal to another tooth. Some are more expensive. Like the big ones in the back—

LEE: So what happened?

AUSTIN: So he locates a Mexican dentist in Juarez who'll do the whole thing for a song. And he takes off hitchhiking to the border.

LEE: Hitchhiking?

AUSTIN: Yeah. So how long you think it takes him to get to the border? A man his age.

LEE: I dunno'.

45

AUSTIN: Eight days it takes him. Eight days in the rain and the
sun and every day he's droppin' teeth on the blacktop and
nobody'll pick him up 'cause his mouth's full a' blood.
(*Pause, they drink.*)
So finally he stumbles into the dentist. Dentist takes all his
money and all his teeth. And there he is, in Mexico, with
his gums sewed up and his pockets empty.
(*Long silence,* AUSTIN *drinks.*)

LEE: That's it?

AUSTIN: Then I go out to see him, see. I go out there and I take
him out for a nice Chinese dinner. But he doesn't eat. All he
wants to do is drink Martinis outa' plastic cups. And he
takes his teeth out and lays 'em on the table 'cause he can't
stand the feel of 'em. And we ask the waitress for one a'
those doggie bags to take the Chop Suey home in. So he
drops his teeth in the doggie bag along with the Chop Suey.
And then we go out to hit all the bars up and down the
highway. Says he wants to introduce me to all his buddies.
And in one a' those bars, in one a' those bars up and down
the highway, he left that doggie bag with his teeth lying in
the Chop Suey.

LEE: You never found it?

AUSTIN: We went back but we never did find it. (*Pause*) Now
that's a true story. True to life.
(*They drink as lights fade to black.*)

SCENE EIGHT

*Very early morning, between night and day, no crickets, coyotes
yapping feverishly in distance before light comes up. A small fire blazes
up in the dark from alcove area, sound of* LEE *smashing typewriter
with a golf club, lights coming up,* LEE *seen smashing typewriter
methodically then dropping pages of his script into a burning bowl set
on the floor of alcove, flames leap up.* AUSTIN *has a whole bunch of
stolen toasters lined up on the sink counter along with Lee's stolen TV.
The toasters are of a wide variety of models, mostly chrome,* AUSTIN
goes up and down the line of toasters, breathing on them and polishing

46

*them with a dish towel. Both men are drunk, empty whiskey bottles
and beer cans litter floor of kitchen, they share a half-empty bottle on
one of the chairs in the alcove,* LEE *keeps periodically taking deliberate
ax-chops at the typewriter, using a nine-iron as* AUSTIN *speaks, all of
their mother's house plants are dead and drooping.*

AUSTIN: *(Polishing toasters)* There's gonna' be a general lack of
   toast in the neighborhood this morning. Many, many
   unhappy, bewildered breakfast faces. I guess it's best not to
   even think of the victims. Not to even entertain it. Is that
   the right psychology?

LEE: *(Pauses)* What?

AUSTIN: Is that the correct criminal psychology? Not to think of
   the victims?

LEE: What victims? *(He takes another swipe at typewriter with
   nine-iron, adds pages to the fire.)*

AUSTIN: The victims of crime. Of breaking and entering. I mean
   is it a prerequisite for a criminal not to have a conscience?

LEE: Ask a criminal *(Pause.* LEE *stares at* AUSTIN.) What're you
   gonna' do with all those toasters? That's the dumbest thing
   I ever saw in my life.

AUSTIN: I've got hundreds of dollars' worth of household
   appliances here. You may not realize that.

LEE: Yeah, and how many hundreds of dollars did you walk right
   past?

AUSTIN: It was toasters you challenged me to. Only toasters. I
   ignored every other temptation.

LEE: I never challenged you! That's no challenge. Anybody can
   steal a toaster. *(He smashes typewriter again.)*

AUSTIN: You don't have to take it out on my typewriter ya' know.
   It's not the machine's fault that you can't write. It's a sin to
   do that to a good machine.

LEE: A sin?

AUSTIN: When you consider all the writers who never even had a
   machine. Who would have given an eyeball for a good
   typewriter. Any typewriter.
   (LEE smashes typewriter again.)
   (Polishing toasters.) All the ones who wrote on matchbook
   covers. Paper bags. Toilet paper. Who had their writing

47

destroyed by their jailers. Who persisted beyond all odds. Those writers would find it hard to understand your actions.

(LEE *comes down on typewriter with one final crushing blow of the nine-iron then collapses in one of the chairs, takes a drink from bottle. Pause*)

(*After pause.*) Not to mention demolishing a perfectly good golf club. What about all the struggling golfers? What about Lee Trevino? What do you think he would've said when he was batting balls around with broom sticks at the age of nine. Impoverished.

(*Pause*)

LEE: What time is it anyway?

AUSTIN: No idea. Time stands still when you're havin' fun.

LEE: Is it too late to call a woman? You know any women?

AUSTIN: I'm a married man.

LEE: I mean a local woman.

(AUSTIN *looks out at light through window above sink.*)

AUSTIN: It's either too late or too early. You're the nature enthusiast. Can't you tell the time by the light in the sky? Orient yourself around the North Star or something?

LEE: I can't tell anything.

AUSTIN: Maybe you need a little breakfast. Some toast! How 'bout some toast?

(AUSTIN *goes to cupboard, pulls out loaf of bread and starts dropping slices into every toaster,* LEE *stays sitting, drinks, watches* AUSTIN.)

LEE: I don't need toast. I need a woman.

AUSTIN: A woman isn't the answer. Never was.

LEE: I'm not talkin' about permanent. I'm talkin' about temporary.

AUSTIN: (*Putting toast in toasters*) We'll just test the merits of these little demons. See which brands have a tendency to burn. See which one can produce a perfectly golden piece of fluffy toast.

LEE: How much gas you got in yer car?

AUSTIN: I haven't driven my car for days now. So I haven't had an opportunity to look at the gas gauge.

LEE: Take a guess. You think there's enough to get me to

48

Bakersfield?

AUSTIN: Bakersfield? What's in Bakersfield?

LEE: Just never mind what's in Bakersfield! You think there's enough goddamn gas in the car!

AUSTIN: Sure.

LEE: Sure. You could care less, right. Let me run outa' gas on the Grapevine. You could give a shit.

AUSTIN: I'd say there was enough gas to get you just about anywhere, Lee. With your determination and guts.

LEE: What the hell time is it anyway?

(LEE *pulls out his wallet, starts going through dozens of small pieces of paper, with phone numbers written on them, drops some on the floor, drops others in the fire.*)

AUSTIN: Very early. This is the time of morning when the coyotes kill people's cocker spaniels. Did you hear them? That's what they were doing out there. Luring innocent pets away from their homes.

LEE: (*Searching through his papers*) What's the area code for Bakersfield? You know?

AUSTIN: You could always call the operator.

LEE: I can't stand that voice they give ya'.

AUSTIN: What voice?

LEE: That voice that warns you that if you'd only tried harder to find the number in the phone book you wouldn't have to be calling the operator to begin with. (*He gets up, holding a slip of paper from his wallet, stumbles toward phone on wall, yanks receiver, starts dialing.*)

AUSTIN: Well I don't understand why you'd want to talk to anybody else anyway. I mean you can talk to me. I'm your brother.

LEE: (*Dialing*) I wanna' talk to a woman. I haven't heard a woman's voice in a long time.

AUSTIN: Not since the Botanist?

LEE: What?

AUSTIN: Nothing. (*Starts singing as he tends toast.*)
Red sails in the sunset
Way out on the blue
Please carry my loved one

D

Home safely to me.

LEE: Hey, knock it off will ya'! This is long distance here.

AUSTIN: Bakersfield?

LEE: Yeah, Bakersfield. It's Kern County.

AUSTIN: Well, what County are *we* in?

LEE: You better get yerself a 7-Up, boy.

AUSTIN: One County's as good as another.

(AUSTIN *hums 'Red Sails' softly as* LEE *talks on phone.*)

LEE: (*To phone*) Yeah, operator, look—first off I wanna' know the area code for Bakersfield. Right. Bakersfield! Okay. Good. Now I wanna' know if you can help me track somebody down. (*Pause*) No, no I mean a phone number. Just a phone number. Okay. (*Holds piece of paper up and reads it.*) Okay, the name is Melly Ferguson. Melly. (*Pause*) I dunno'. Melly. Maybe. Yeah. Maybe Melanie. Yeah. Melanie Ferguson. Okay. (*Pause*) What? I can't hear ya' so good. Sounds like yer under the ocean. (*Pause*) You got ten Melanie Fergusons? How could that be? Ten Melanie Fergusons in Bakersfield? Well gimme all of 'em then. (*Pause*) What d'ya' mean? Gimme all ten Melanie Fergusons! That's right. Just a second. (*To* AUSTIN.) Gimme a pen.

AUSTIN: I don't have a pen.

LEE: Gimme a pencil then!

AUSTIN: I don't have a pencil.

LEE: (*To phone*) Just a second, operator. (*To* AUSTIN.) Yer a writer and ya' don't have a pen or a pencil!

AUSTIN: I'm not a writer. You're a writer.

LEE: I'm on the phone here! Get me a pen or a pencil.

AUSTIN: I gotta' watch the toast.

LEE: (*To phone*) Hang on a second, operator.

(LEE *lets the phone drop then starts pulling all the drawers in the kitchen out on the floor and dumping the contents, searching for a pencil,* AUSTIN *watches him casually.*)

(*Crashing through drawers, throwing contents around kitchen.*) This is the last time I try to live with people, boy! I can't believe it. Here I am! Here I am again in a desperate situation! This would never happen out on the desert. I would never be in this kinda' situation out on the desert.

Isn't there a pen or pencil in this house! Who lives in this house anyway!

AUSTIN: Our mother.

LEE: How come she don't have a pen or a pencil! She's a social person isn't she? Doesn't she have to make shopping lists? She's gotta' have a pencil. (*Finds a pencil.*) Aaha! (*He rushes back to phone, picks up receiver.*) All right, operator. Operator? Hey! Operator! Goddamnit! (*He rips the phone off the wall and throws it down, goes back to chair and falls into it, drinks. Long pause.*)

AUSTIN: She hung up?

LEE: Yeah, she hung up. I knew she was gonna' hang up. I could hear it in her voice. (*He starts going through his slips of paper again.*)

AUSTIN: Well, you're probably better off staying here with me anyway. I'll take care of you.

LEE: I don't need takin' care of! Not by you anyway.

AUSTIN: Toast is almost ready. (*He starts buttering all the toast as it pops up.*)

LEE: I don't want any toast!

(*Long pause.*)

AUSTIN: You gotta' eat something. Can't just drink. How long have we been drinking, anyway?

LEE: (*Looking through slips of paper*) Maybe it was Fresno. What's the area code for Fresno? How could I have lost that number! She was beautiful.

(*Pause*)

AUSTIN: Why don't you just forget about that, Lee. Forget about the woman.

LEE: She had green eyes. You know what green eyes do to me?

AUSTIN: I know but you're not gonna' get it on with her now anyway. It's dawn already. She's in Bakersfield for Christ's sake.

(*Long pause, LEE considers the situation.*)

LEE: Yeah. (*Looks at windows.*) It's dawn!

AUSTIN: Let's just have some toast and—

LEE: What is this bullshit with the toast anyway! You make it sound like salvation or something. I don't want any goddamn

51

toast! How many times I gotta' tell ya'!

(LEE *gets up, crosses up stage to windows in alcove, looks out.* AUSTIN *butters toast.*)

AUSTIN: Well it is like salvation sort of. I mean the smell. I love the smell of toast. And the sun's coming up. It makes me feel like anything's possible. Ya' know?

LEE: (*Back to* AUSTIN, *facing windows up stage*) So go to church why don't ya'.

AUSTIN: Like a beginning. I love beginnings.

LEE: Oh yeah. I've always been kinda' partial to endings myself.

AUSTIN: What if I come with you, Lee?

LEE: (*Pause as* LEE *turns toward* AUSTIN) What?

AUSTIN: What if I come with you out to the desert?

LEE: Are you kiddin'?

AUSTIN: No. I'd just like to see what it's like.

LEE: You wouldn't last a day out there pal.

AUSTIN: That's what you said about the toasters. You said I couldn't steal a toaster either.

LEE: A toaster's got nothin' to do with the desert.

AUSTIN: I could make it, Lee. I'm not that helpless. I can cook.

LEE: Cook?

AUSTIN: I can.

LEE: So what! You can cook. Toast.

AUSTIN: I can make fires. I know how to get fresh water from condensation.

(AUSTIN *stacks buttered toast up in a tall stack on plate.* LEE *slams table.*)

LEE: It's not somethin' you learn out of a Boy Scout Handbook!

AUSTIN: Well how do you learn it then! How're you supposed to learn it!

(*Pause*)

LEE: Ya' just learn it, that's all. Ya' learn it 'cause ya' have to learn it. You don't *have* to learn it.

AUSTIN: You could teach me.

LEE: (*Stands*) What're you, crazy or somethin'? You went to college. Here, you are down here, rollin' in bucks. Floatin' up and down in elevators. And you wanna' learn how to live on the desert!

52

AUSTIN: I do, Lee. I really do. There's nothin' down here for me. There never was. When we were kids here it was different. There was a life here then. But now—I keep comin' down here thinkin' it's the fifties or somethin'. I keep finding myself getting off the freeway at familiar landmarks that turn out to be unfamiliar. On the way to appointments. Wandering down streets I thought I recognized that turn out to be replicas of streets I remember. Streets I misremember. Streets I can't tell if I lived on or saw in a postcard. Fields that don't even exist anymore.

LEE: There's no point cryin' about that now.

AUSTIN: There's nothin' real down here, Lee! Least of all me!

LEE: Well I can't save you from that!

AUSTIN: You can let me come with you.

LEE: No dice, pal.

AUSTIN: You could let me come with you, Lee!

LEE: Hey, do you actually think I chose to live out in the middle a' nowhere? Do ya'? Ya' think it's some kinda' philosophical decision I took or somethin'? I'm livin' out there 'cause I can't make it here! And yer bitchin' to me about all yer success!

AUSTIN: I'd cash it all in in a second. That's the truth.

LEE: (*Pause, shakes his head*) I can't believe this.

AUSTIN: Let me go with you.

LEE: Stop sayin' that will ya'! Yer worse than a dog.

(AUSTIN *offers out the plate of neatly stacked toast to* LEE.)

AUSTIN: You want some toast?

(LEE *suddenly explodes and knocks the plate out of* AUSTIN's *hand, toast goes flying. Long frozen moment where it appears* LEE *might go all the way this time when* AUSTIN *breaks it by slowly lowering himself to his knees and begins gathering the scattered toast from the floor and stacking it back on the plate.* LEE *begins to circle* AUSTIN *in a slow, predatory way, crushing pieces of toast in his wake, no words for a while.* AUSTIN *keeps gathering toast, even the crushed pieces.*)

LEE: Tell ya' what I'll do little brother. I might just consider makin' you a deal. Little trade.

(AUSTIN *continues gathering toast as* LEE *circles him through this.*)

You write me up this screenplay thing just like I tell ya'. I mean you can use all yer usual tricks and stuff. Yer fancy language. Yer artistic hocus pocus. But ya' gotta' write everything like I say. Every move. Every time they run outa' gas, they run outa' gas. Every time they wanna' jump on a horse, they do just that. If they wanna' stay in Texas, by God they'll stay in Texas! (*Keeps circling.*) And you finish the whole thing up for me. Top to bottom. And you put my name on it. And I own all the rights. And every dime goes in my pocket. You do all that and I'll sure enough take ya' with me to the desert. (LEE *stops, pause, looks down at* AUSTIN.) How's that sound?

(*Pause as* AUSTIN *stands slowly, holding plate of demolished toast. Their faces are very close, pause.*)

AUSTIN: It's a deal.

(LEE *stares straight into* AUSTIN's *eyes, then he slowly takes a piece of toast off the plate, raises it to his mouth and takes a huge crushing bite, never taking his eyes off* AUSTIN's. *As* LEE *crunches into the toast the lights black out.*)

SCENE NINE

Mid-day, no sound, blazing heat, the stage is ravaged; bottles, toasters, smashed typewriter, ripped out telephone, etc. All the debris from previous scene is now starkly visible in intense yellow light; the effect should be like a desert junkyard at high noon, the coolness of the preceding scenes is totally obliterated. AUSTIN *is seated at table in alcove, shirt open, pouring with sweat, hunched over a writing notebook, scribbling notes desperately with a ballpoint pen.* LEE *with no shirt, beer in hand, sweat pouring down his chest, is walking a slow circle around the table, picking his way through the objects, sometimes kicking them aside.*

LEE: (*As he walks*) All right, read it back to me. Read it back to me!

AUSTIN: (*Scribbling at top speed*) Just a second.

LEE: Come on, come on! Just read what ya' got.

AUSTIN: I can't keep up! It's not the same as if I had a typewriter.

LEE: Just read what we got so far. Forget about the rest.

AUSTIN: All right. Let's see—okay—

(AUSTIN *wipes sweat from his face, reads as* LEE *circles.*)

Luke says uh—

LEE: Luke?

AUSTIN: Yeah.

LEE: His name's Luke? All right, all right—we can change the names later. What's he say? Come on, come on.

AUSTIN: He says uh— (*Reading*) 'I told ya' you were a fool to follow me in here. I know this prairie like the back a' my hand.'

LEE: No, no, no! That's not what I said. I never said that.

AUSTIN: That's what I wrote.

LEE: It's not what I said. I never said 'like the back a' my hand'. That's stupid. That's one a' those—whadya' call it? Whadya' call that?

AUSTIN: What?

LEE: Whadya' call it when somethin's been said a thousand times before. Whadya' call that?

AUSTIN: Um—a cliché?

LEE: Yeah. That's right. Cliché. That's what that is. A cliché. 'The back a' my hand'. That's stupid.

AUSTIN: That's what you said.

LEE: I never said that! And even if I did, that's where yer supposed to come in. That's where yer supposed to change it to somethin' better.

AUSTIN: Well how am I supposed to do that and write down what you say at the same time?

LEE: Ya' just do, that's all! You hear a stupid line you change it. That's yer job.

AUSTIN: All right. (*Makes more notes.*)

LEE: What're you changin' it to?

AUSTIN: I'm not changing it. I'm just trying to catch up.

LEE: Well change it! We gotta' change that, we can't leave that in there like that. '. . . the back a' my hand'. That's dumb.

AUSTIN: (*Stops writing, sits back*) All right.

LEE: (*Pacing*) So what'll we change it to?

AUSTIN: Um— How 'bout—'I'm on intimate terms with this prairie.'

LEE: (*To himself, considering line as he walks*) 'I'm on intimate terms with this prairie.' Intimate terms, intimate terms. Intimate—that means like uh—sexual, right?

AUSTIN: Well—yeah—or—

LEE: He's on sexual terms with the prairie? How dya' figure that?

AUSTIN: Well it doesn't necessarily have to mean sexual.

LEE: What's it mean then?

AUSTIN: It means uh—close—personal—

LEE: All right. How's it sound? Put it into the uh—the line there. Read it back. Let's see how it sounds. (*To himself.*) 'Intimate terms'.

AUSTIN: (*Scribbles in notebook*) Okay. It'd go something like this: (*Reads*) 'I told ya' you were a fool to follow me in here. I'm on intimate terms with this prairie.'

LEE: That's good. I like that. That's real good.

AUSTIN: You do?

LEE: Yeah. Don't you?

AUSTIN: Sure.

LEE: Sounds original now. 'Intimate terms'. That's good. Okay. Now we're cookin'! That has a real ring to it.

(AUSTIN *makes more notes,* LEE *walks around, pours beer on his arms and rubs it over his chest feeling good about the new progress. As he does this* MOM *enters unobtrusively down stage left with her luggage. She stops and stares at the scene, still holding luggage, as the two men continue, unaware of her presence,* AUSTIN *absorbed in his writing,* LEE *cooling himself off with beer.* LEE *continues.*)

'He's on intimate terms with this prairie.' Sounds real mysterious and kinda' threatening at the same time.

AUSTIN: (*Writing rapidly*) Good.

LEE: Now—

(LEE *turns and suddenly sees* MOM, *he stares at her for a while, she stares back,* AUSTIN *keeps writing feverishly, not noticing.* LEE *walks slowly over to* MOM *and takes a closer look. Long*

56

pause.)

Mom?

(AUSTIN *looks up suddenly from his writing, sees* MOM, *stands quickly, long pause.* MOM *surveys the damage.)*

AUSTIN: Mom. What're you doing back?

MOM: I'm back.

LEE: Here, lemme take those for ya'.

(LEE *sets beer on counter then takes both her bags, but doesn't know where to set them down in the sea of junk so he just keeps holding them.)*

AUSTIN: I wasn't expecting you back so soon. I thought uh—
How was Alaska?

MOM: Fine.

LEE: See any igloos?

MOM: No, Just glaciers.

AUSTIN: Cold, huh?

MOM: What?

AUSTIN: It must've been cold up there?

MOM: Not really.

LEE: Musta' been colder than this here. I mean we're havin' a real scorcher here.

MOM: Oh? (*She looks at damage.*)

LEE: Yeah. Must be in the hundreds.

AUSTIN: You wanna' take your coat off, Mom?

MOM: No. (*Pause, she surveys space.*) What happened in here?

AUSTIN: Oh um— Me and Lee were just sort of celebrating and uh—

MOM: Celebrating?

AUSTIN: Yeah. Uh—Lee sold a screenplay. A story, I mean.

MOM: Lee did?

AUSTIN: Yeah.

MOM: Not you?

AUSTIN: No. Him.

MOM: (*To* LEE) You sold a screenplay?

LEE: Yeah. That's right. We're just sorta' finishing it up ri now. That's what we're doing here.

AUSTIN: Me and Lee are going out to the desert to live.

MOM: You and Lee?

57

AUSTIN: Yeah. I'm taking off with Lee.

MOM: (*She looks back and forth at each of them. Pause*) You gonna' go live with your father?

AUSTIN: No. We're going to a different desert, Mom.

MOM: I see. Well, you'll probably wind up on the same desert sooner or later. What're all these toasters doing here?

AUSTIN: Well—we had a kind of contest.

MOM: Contest?

LEE: Yeah.

AUSTIN: Lee won.

MOM: Did you win a lot of money, Lee?

LEE: Well, not yet. It's comin' in any day now.

MOM: (*To* LEE) What happened to your shirt?

LEE: Oh. I was sweatin' like a pig and I took it off.

(AUSTIN *grabs* LEE's *shirt off the table and tosses it to him.* LEE *sets down suitcases and puts his shirt on.*)

MOM: Well it's one hell of a mess in here isn't it?

AUSTIN: Yeah, I'll clean it up for you, Mom. I just didn't know you were coming back so soon.

MOM: I didn't either.

AUSTIN: What happened?

MOM: Nothing. I just started missing all my plants. (*She notices dead plants.*)

AUSTIN: Oh.

MOM: Oh, they're all dead aren't they. (*She crosses toward them, examines them closely.*) You didn't get a chance to water, I guess.

AUSTIN: I was doing it and then Lee came and—

LEE: Yeah I just distracted him a whole lot here, Mom. It's not his fault.

(*Pause, as* MOM *stares at plants.*)

MOM: Oh well, one less thing to take care of I guess. (*Turns toward brothers.*) Oh, that reminds me— You boys will probably never guess who's in town. Try and guess.

(*Long pause, brothers stare at her.*)

AUSTIN: Whadya' mean, Mom?

MOM: Take a guess. Somebody very important has come to town. I read it, coming down on the Greyhound.

LEE: Somebody very important?

MOM: See if you can guess. You'll never guess.

AUSTIN: Mom— we're trying to uh— (*Points to writing pad.*)

MOM: Picasso. (*Pause*) Picasso's in town. Isn't that incredible? Right now.

(*Pause*)

AUSTIN: Picasso's dead, Mom.

MOM: No, he's not dead. He's visiting the museum. I read it on the bus. We have to go down there and see him.

AUSTIN: Mom—

MOM: This is the chance of a lifetime. Can you imagine? We could all go down and meet him. All three of us.

LEE: Uh— I don't think I'm really up fer meetin' anybody right now. I'm uh— What's his name?

MOM: Picasso! Picasso! You've never heard of Picasso? Austin, you've heard of Picasso.

AUSTIN: Mom, we're not going to have time.

MOM: It won't take long. We'll just hop in the car and go down there. An opportunity like this doesn't come along every day.

AUSTIN: We're gonna' be leavin' here, Mom!

(*Pause*)

MOM: Oh.

LEE: Yeah.

(*Pause*)

MOM: You're both leaving?

LEE: (*Looks at* AUSTIN) Well we were thinkin' about that before but now I—

AUSTIN: No, we are! We're both leaving. We've got it all planned.

MOM: (*To* AUSTIN) Well you can't leave. You have a family.

AUSTIN: I'm leaving. I'm getting out of here.

LEE: (*To* MOM) I don't really think Austin's cut out for the desert, do you?

MOM: No. He's not.

AUSTIN: I'm going with you, Lee!

MOM: He's too thin.

LEE: Yeah, he'd just burn up out there.

AUSTIN: (*To* LEE) We just gotta' finish this screenplay and then

59

we're gonna' take off. That's the plan. That's what you said. Come on, let's get back to work, Lee.

LEE: I can't work under these conditions here. It's too hot.

AUSTIN: Then we'll do it on the desert.

LEE: Don't be tellin' me what we're gonna' do!

MOM: Don't shout in the house.

LEE: We're just gonna' have to postpone the whole deal.

AUSTIN: I can't postpone it! It's gone past postponing! I'm doing everything you said. I'm writing down exactly what you tell me.

LEE: Yeah, but you were right all along see. It is a dumb story. 'Two lamebrains chasin' each other across Texas.' That's what you said, right?

AUSTIN: I never said that.

(LEE *sneers in* AUSTIN's *face, then turns to* MOM.)

LEE: I'm gonna' just borrow some a' your antiques, Mom. You don't mind do ya'? Just a few plates and things. Silverware.

(LEE *starts going through all the cupboards in the kitchen, pulling out plates and stacking them on counter as* MOM *and* AUSTIN *watch.*)

MOM: You don't have any utensils on the desert?

LEE: Nah, I'm fresh out.

AUSTIN: (*To* LEE) What're you doing?

MOM: Well some of those are very old. Bone china.

LEE: I'm tired of eatin' outa' my bare hands, ya' know. It's not civilized.

AUSTIN: (*To* LEE) What're you doing? We made a deal!

MOM: Couldn't you borrow the plastic ones instead? I have plenty of plastic ones.

LEE: (*As he stacks plates*) It's not the same. Plastic's not the same at all. What I need is somethin' authentic. Somethin' to keep me in touch. It's easy to get outa' touch out there. Don't worry I'll get 'em back to ya'.

(AUSTIN *rushes up to* LEE, *grabs him by shoulders.*)

AUSTIN: You can't just drop the whole thing, Lee!

(LEE *turns, pushes* AUSTIN *in the chest, knocking him backwards into the alcove.* MOM *watches numbly,* LEE *returns to collecting the plates, silverware, etc.*)

60

MOM: You boys shouldn't fight in the house. Go outside and fight.

LEE: I'm not fightin'. I'm leavin'.

MOM: There's been enough damage done already.

LEE: (*His back to* AUSTIN *and* MOM, *stacking dishes on counter*) I'm clearin' outa' here once and for all. All this town does is drive a man insane. Look what it's done to Austin there. I'm not lettin' that happen to me. Sell myself down the river. No sir. I'd rather be a hundred miles from nowhere than let that happen to me.

(*During this*, AUSTIN *has picked up the ripped-out phone from the floor and wrapped the cord tightly around both his hands. He lunges at* LEE *whose back is still to him, wraps the cord around* LEE's *neck, plants a foot in* LEE's *back and pulls back on the cord, tightening it.* LEE *chokes desperately, can't speak and can't reach* AUSTIN *with his arms.* AUSTIN *keeps applying pressure on* LEE's *back with his foot, bending him into the sink.* MOM *watches.*)

AUSTIN: (*Tightening cord*) You're not goin' anywhere! You're not takin' anything with you. You're not takin' my car! You're not takin' the dishes! You're not takin' anything! You're stayin' right here!

MOM: You'll have to stop fighting in the house. There's plenty of room outside to fight. You've got the whole outdoors to fight in.

(LEE *tries to tear himself away. He crashes across the stage like an enraged bull, dragging* AUSTIN *with him. He snorts and bellows but* AUSTIN *hangs on and manages to keep clear of* LEE's *attempts to grab him. They crash into the table, to the floor.* LEE *is face down thrashing wildly and choking,* AUSTIN *pulls cord tighter, stands with one foot planted on* LEE's *back and the cord stretched taut.*)

AUSTIN: (*Holding cord*) Gimme back my keys, Lee! Take the keys out! Take 'em out!

(LEE *desperately tries to dig in his pockets, searching for the car keys.* MOM *moves closer.*)

MOM: (*Calmly to* AUSTIN) You're not killing him are you?

AUSTIN: I don't know. I don't know if I'm killing him. I'm

61

stopping him. That's all. I'm just stopping him.

(LEE *thrashes but* AUSTIN *is relentless.*)

MOM: You oughta' let him breathe a little bit.

AUSTIN: Throw the keys out, Lee!

(LEE *finally gets keys out and throws them on floor but out of*
AUSTIN's *reach.* AUSTIN *keeps pressure on cord, pulling* LEE's *neck*
back. LEE *gets one hand to the cord but can't relieve the pressure.*)
Reach me those keys would ya', Mom?

MOM: (*Not moving*) Why are you doing this to him?

AUSTIN: Reach me the keys!

MOM: Not until you stop choking him.

AUSTIN: I can't stop choking him! He'll kill me if I stop choking him!

MOM: He won't kill you. He's your brother.

AUSTIN: Just get me the keys would ya'!

(*Pause.* MOM *picks keys off floor, hands them to* AUSTIN.)

(*To* MOM.) Thanks.

MOM: Will you let him go now?

AUSTIN: I don't know. He's not gonna' let me get outa' here.

MOM: Well you can't kill him.

AUSTIN: I can kill him! I can easily kill him. Right now. Right
here. All I gotta' do is just tighten up. See?

(AUSTIN *tightens cord,* LEE *thrashes wildly,* AUSTIN *releases*
pressure a little, maintaining control.)
Ya' see that?

MOM: That's a savage thing to do.

AUSTIN: Yeah well don't tell me I can't kill him, because I can. I
can just twist. I can keep twisting.

(AUSTIN *twists the cord tighter,* LEE *weakens, his breathing*
changes to a short rasp.)

MOM: Austin!

(AUSTIN *relieves pressure,* LEE *breathes easier but* AUSTIN *keeps*
him under control.)

AUSTIN: (*Eyes on* LEE, *holding cord*) I'm goin' to the desert.
There's nothing stopping me. I'm going by myself to the
desert.

MOM: (*Moving toward her luggage*) Well, I'm going to go check
into a motel. I can't stand this anymore.

AUSTIN: Don't go yet!

(MOM *pauses*.)

MOM: I can't stay here. This is worse than being homeless.

AUSTIN: I'll get everything fixed up for you, Mom. I promise. Just stay for a while.

MOM: (*Picking up luggage*) You're going to the desert.

AUSTIN: Just wait!

(LEE *thrashes*, AUSTIN *subdues him*, MOM *watches, holding luggage. Pause*)

MOM: It was the worst feeling being up there. In Alaska. Staring out a window. I never felt so desperate before. That's why when I saw that article on Picasso I thought—

AUSTIN: Stay here, Mom. This is where you live.

(MOM *looks around the stage*.)

MOM: I don't recognize it at all.

(MOM *exits with luggage*, AUSTIN *makes a move toward her but* LEE *starts to struggle and* AUSTIN *subdues him again with cord. Pause*)

AUSTIN: (*Holding cord*) Lee? I'll make ya' a deal. You let me get outa' here. Just let me get to my car. All right, Lee? Gimme a little headstart and I'll turn you loose. Just gimme a little headstart. All right?

(LEE *makes no response*, AUSTIN *slowly releases tension on cord, still nothing from* LEE.)

Lee?

(LEE *is motionless*, AUSTIN *very slowly begins to stand, still keeping a tenuous hold on the cord and his eyes riveted to* LEE *for any sign of movement.* AUSTIN *slowly drops the cord and stands, he stares down at* LEE *who appears to be dead*.)

(*Whispers*) Lee?

(*Pause.* AUSTIN *considers, looks toward exit, back to* LEE, *then makes a small movement as if to leave. Instantly* LEE *is on his feet and moves toward exit, blocking* AUSTIN's *escape. They square off to each other, keeping a distance between them. Pause. A single coyote heard in distance, lights fade softly into moonlight, the figures of the brothers now appear to be caught in a vast desert-like landscape. They are very still but watchful for the next move. Lights go slowly to black as the after-image of the brothers pulses in the dark, coyote fades*.)